Birding hotspots in the Algarve

Around Lagos

Gonçalo Elias

Birding hotspots in the Algarve

Around Lagos

Title:	Birding hotspots in the Algarve: Around Lagos
Author:	Gonçalo Elias
Cover page:	Dartford Warbler *Sylvia undata* (Pedro Marques)
Digital illustrations:	C. Maria Elias
Production:	C. Maria Elias
Printing:	Createspace.com
Distribution:	Amazon.com

1st edition, May 2016

ISBN: 978-1533085542

Print On Demand

Contact: goncalo.elias@gmail.com

CONTENTS

Lagos

Situated on the coast in the western Algarve, Lagos is a popular tourist town. The concelho (municipality) of Lagos covers an area of 214 km². It is bordered by the Atlantic Ocean to the south, by the Alvor estuary to the east, by the coastal village of Burgau to the west and by a small chain of hills called Serra de Espinhaço de Cão to the north.

This concelho has very diverse habitats – there are two small coastal wetlands (Lagos marsh and Alvor estuary), coastal cliffs, small forest patches and scrub-covered hills.

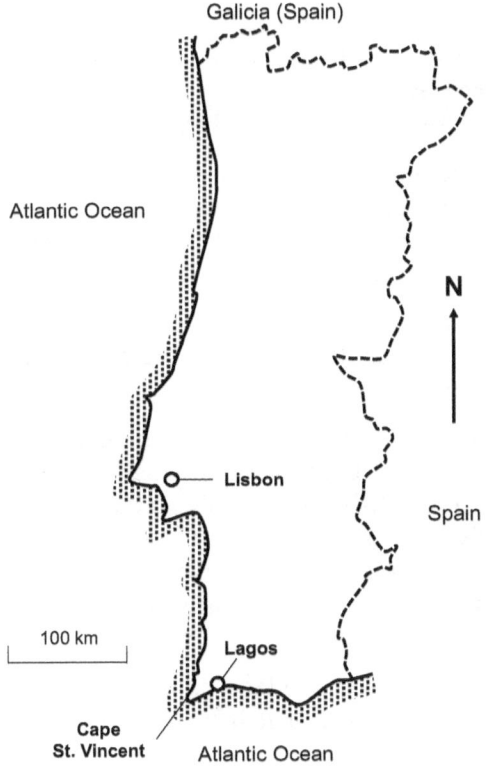

Map of Portugal showing the location of Lagos and the capital Lisbon

Birding around Lagos

Lagos is often overlooked in birdwatching guides, which tend to focus on large, well-known sites elsewhere in the Algarve and so it is easy to miss this area altogether. However, for the visiting birdwatcher, the concelho of Lagos certainly deserves some attention. Indeed, it is not necessary to go very far to see many different birds: over 260 bird species have been recorded in Lagos concelho alone!

In this booklet we present a number of birding hotspots in the concelho of Lagos, aiming at helping anyone with an interest in birds to get the best birding opportunities. Hotspot selection has been made taking into account bird variety and ease of access.

A short description is provided for each hotspot, along with a list of the most interesting birds to be found there and some suggestions of how it can be explored. Some species that are common throughout the region, such as Goldfinch or Blackbird, have been left out.

West of the town the coast is rocky. A large promontory stands out – it is called **Ponta da Piedade**. This location has imposing cliffs and is the best spot near Lagos for seawatching. There are also some cliff-nesting birds, like Blue Rock Thrush, and passage migrants.

In the middle of the town, it is worth looking at the **Lagos harbour**. This place often attracts gulls and terns, while the surrounding areas often have passerines, especially on passage.

Not far from Lagos, there is an aerodrome and next to it there is a small wetland, informally called **Lagos marsh**, which includes some patches of reeds and also a few fish ponds. This wetland often attracts some waterbirds, mostly waders, egrets and birds of reedbeds. A few kilometres eastwards lies another interesting place for waterbirds: the **Odiáxere saltpans**. Waders are regularly seen, and there are often Flamingos (uncommon in this part of the Algarve).

Finally, we reach the largest wetland in the concelho of Lagos: the Alvor estuary. Although most of it belongs to Portimão, the western shore called **Vale da Lama** is part of Lagos. There are tidal mudflats, which attract a variety of waders, gulls, terns and other waterbirds.

The inland areas are hilly and largely covered with scrub, mainly Gum Rockrose, but there are also some forest patches. **Barão de São João** is a large pinewood, which attracts some forest birds. This location is also a good spot from where to watch raptor migration in autumn. **Catalão** is a more open site, where it is possible to find a mix of open country birds, especially larks, but raptors can also be seen on passage. Further north, along the road to Aljezur, lies the Serra de Espinhaço de Cão, a hilly area covered mainly with cork oaks; it can be explored at places like **Pincho** – there is a good variety of forest birds, including Redstart, Iberian Chiffchaff, Firecrest, Cirl Bunting, and wintering Bullfinch. Finally, the area around **Bravura dam** is open and covered with scrub, so it is best for passerines such as *Sylvia* warblers. The dam wall has Blue Rock Thrush.

Although a car is useful for getting around, it should be noted that most hotspots in the concelho of Lagos can be reached using public transport. More details about this option are provided at the end.

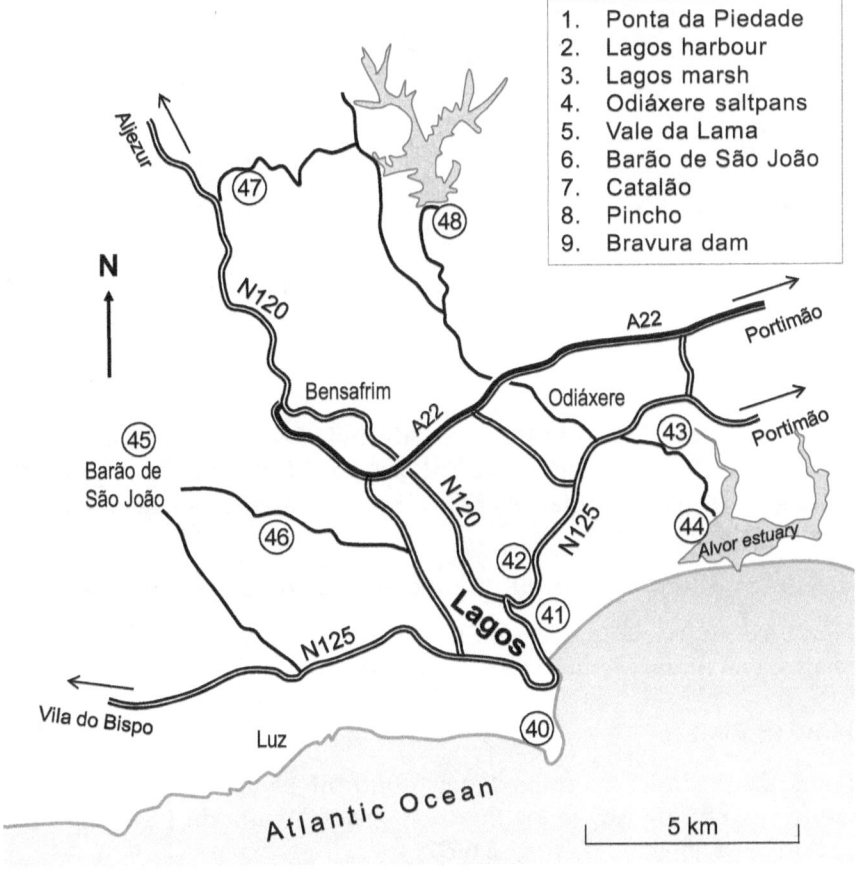

1. Ponta da Piedade
2. Lagos harbour
3. Lagos marsh
4. Odiáxere saltpans
5. Vale da Lama
6. Barão de São João
7. Catalão
8. Pincho
9. Bravura dam

Map of birding hotspots in the concelho of Lagos

9

Ponta da Piedade

A beautiful area formed by golden cliffs, sheltered beaches and small rocky islets.

Birds

Resident: Cattle Egret, Little Egret, Kestrel, Peregrine, Yellow-legged Gull, Rock Pigeon, Crested Lark, Black Redstart, Blue Rock Thrush, Zitting Cisticola, Sardinian Warbler, Iberian Magpie, Jackdaw, Spotless Starling, Corn Bunting

Breeding visitors: Pallid Swift, Alpine Swift, Red-rumped Swallow

Non-breeding visitors: Cory's Shearwater, Gannet, Great Cormorant, Shag, Great Skua, Mediterranean Gull, Northern Wheatear

How to visit it

Ponta da Piedade lies immediately south of Lagos town and can be easily reached by car, following the signs to 'Ponta da Piedade'. Free parking is available (37.0818, -8.6697).

The best way to visit this place is on foot. However, extra care should be taken when walking near the cliffs, as there are no protections.

To get a good view of the cliffs, the best approach is to walk around the lighthouse. The cliffs themselves usually hold Rock Pigeon (of the wild type), Black Redstart and Blue Rock Thrush. A few Jackdaws still occur here, although numbers have dropped markedly in the last 20 years. Peregrine breeds along the coast and is a regular sight at this location. The adjacent islets are used by Yellow-legged Gulls, Spotless Starlings and, in winter, by a few Cormorants and sometimes Shags.

Seawatching can be rewarding, with Gannets, Great Skuas and Cory's Shearwaters among the most regular species.

To the north lies a small plateau, which has a few land birds, including Crested Lark, Zitting Cisticola, Sardinian Warbler and Iberian Magpie. During passage periods, this plateau is a good place to look for migrant passerines. It can be explored on foot using one of the many footpaths.

Lagos harbour

A small fishing harbour on the left bank of river Bensafrim, surrounded by dunes and a small pond.

Birds

Resident: Little Grebe, Little Egret, Moorhen, Coot, Yellow-legged Gull, Crested Lark, Zitting Cisticola, Serin, Linnet

Breeding visitors: Common Swift

Non-breeding visitors: Great Cormorant, Common Sandpiper, Turnstone, Mediterranean Gull, Black-headed Gull, Lesser Black-backed Gull, Sandwich Tern, Kingfisher, Crag Martin, Bluethroat, Northern Wheatear, Spanish Sparrow

How to visit it

The harbour is very easy to find, as it lies next to the Lagos railway station. Free parking is available close to the harbour (37.1074, -8.6733).

On a typical winter day, it is possible to see a few Yellow-legged, Lesser Black-backed and Black-headed Gulls, along with Cormorant, Sandwich Tern, the odd Little Egret and a few waders.

However, during periods of bad weather, the number of gulls can be higher. Additionally, other species, notably gulls and terns, occasionally turn up on passage.

The dunes lie on the south side and separate the harbour from the sea. They are home to Crested Lark, Zitting Cisticola, Serin and Linnet, but in spring and autumn, they sometimes attract other migrants, including Short-toed Lark and Northern Wheatear. Snow Bunting has been seen in winter.

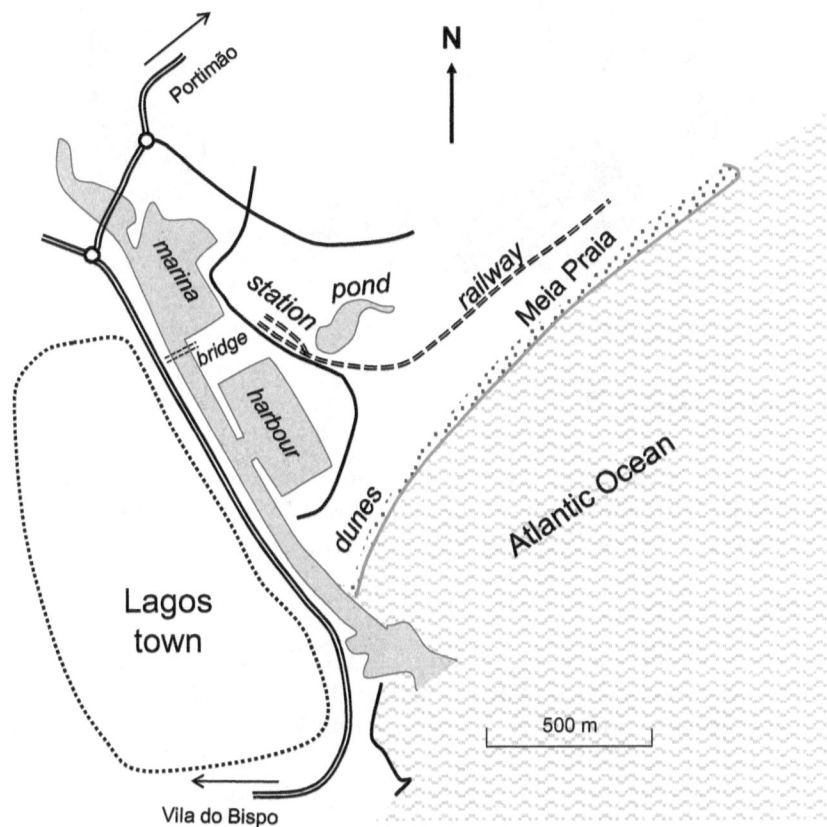

From the southern tip of the train station, it is possible to look at the nearby pond, which lies on the other side of the railway (a telescope is useful here). Common birds include Mallard, Coot, Moorhen and Little Grebe, along with hirundines. However, winter brings a few interesting passerines, including Crag Martin, Bluethroat and sometimes Spanish Sparrow.

Lagos marsh

A marshy area, also known as 'Paul de Lagos', with extensive reedbeds, saltmarsh a set of old fish ponds. In the surroundings, there are some patches of Cork Oak and Umbrella Pine.

Birds

Resident: Quail, Cattle Egret, Little Egret, White Stork, Black-winged Kite, Marsh Harrier, Water Rail, Black-winged Stilt, Hoopoe, Iberian Green Woodpecker, Lesser Spotted Woodpecker, Crested Lark, Cetti's Warbler, Zitting Cisticola, Sardinian Warbler, Iberian Magpie, Spotless Starling, Waxbill, Serin, Linnet, Hawfinch, Corn Bunting

Breeding visitors: Little Ringed Plover, Common Swift, Pallid Swift, Bee-eater, Red-rumped Swallow, Nightingale, Reed Warbler, Iberian Chiffchaff

Non-breeding visitors: Teal, Great Egret, Glossy Ibis, Spoonbill, Ringed Plover, Lapwing, Common Redshank, Greenshank, Green Sandpiper, Common Sandpiper, Dunlin, Common Snipe, Whimbrel, Skylark, Crag Martin, Water Pipit, Bluethroat, Penduline Tit

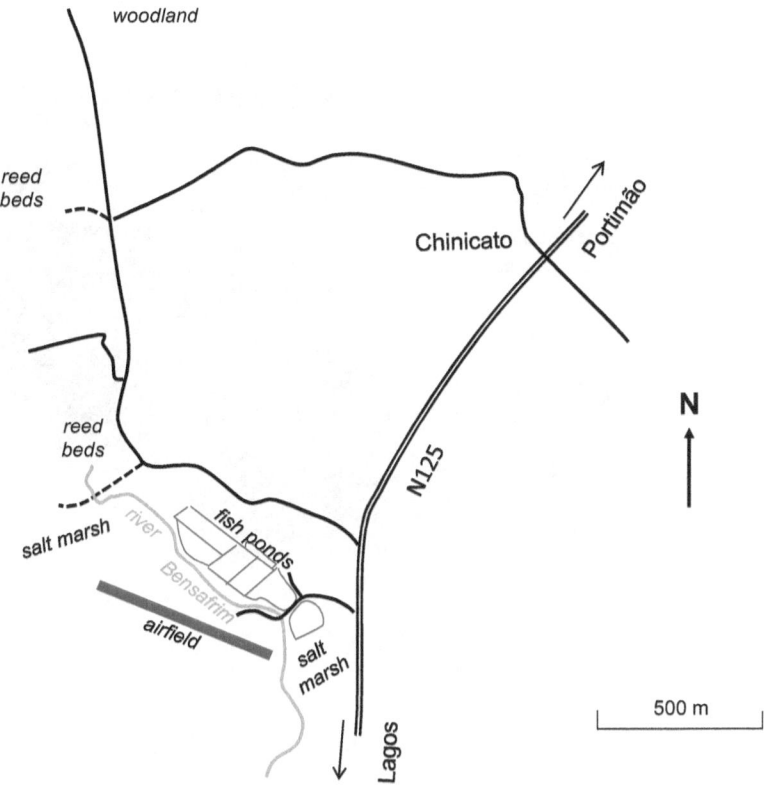

How to visit it

There are three main areas worth inspecting: the fish ponds, the reedbeds and the woodland.

The fish ponds are located next to the airfield and can be approached by car (leave Lagos eastwards on the N125 and turn left after 1 km following the signs to 'aeródromo'). This is a good spot to look for waterbirds, namely waders, gulls and egrets (37.1224, -8.6753).

Back on the N125, veer left where signposted 'Sargaçal' and proceed for about 1 km until a reedbed appears on the left. Park where possible and explore. Breeding birds here include Marsh Harrier, Water Rail, Cetti's and Reed Warblers, whereas Water Pipit, Bluethroat and Penduline Tit occur in winter.

About 1 km further north there is a patch of mixed woodland on the right side of the road – here it is possible to find several forest birds, including woodpeckers and Hawfinch.

Odiáxere saltpans

A small set of abandoned saltpans, close to river Odiáxere. Part of the surrounding area is covered by saltmarsh.

Birds

Resident: Little Egret, White Stork, Black-winged Kite, Black-winged Stilt, Crested Lark, Zitting Cisticola, Iberian Magpie, Spotless Starling, Serin, Linnet, Waxbill

Breeding visitors: Little Ringed Plover, Common Swift, Pallid Swift, Bee-eater, Red-rumped Swallow

Non-breeding visitors: Flamingo, Grey Heron, Spoonbill, Glossy Ibis, Marsh Harrier, Peregrine, Ringed Plover, Lapwing, Common Redshank, Greenshank, Green Sandpiper, Dunlin, Common Snipe, Crag Martin, Bluethroat, Water Pipit, Spanish Sparrow

How to visit it

Leave Lagos eastwards on the N125. Just after passing Odiáxere, veer right on the small road signposted 'Vale da Lama'. After about 1 km, the saltpans appear on the roadside (37.1483, -8.6434).

The place is not fenced and can be visited on foot. It should be noted that there are tanks on both sides of the road. The western (southern) complex can be easily seen from the car. As to the eastern complex, it can be approached by following a track that runs along its south side and also offers a view over the saltmarsh (this track is sometimes muddy, especially in winter).

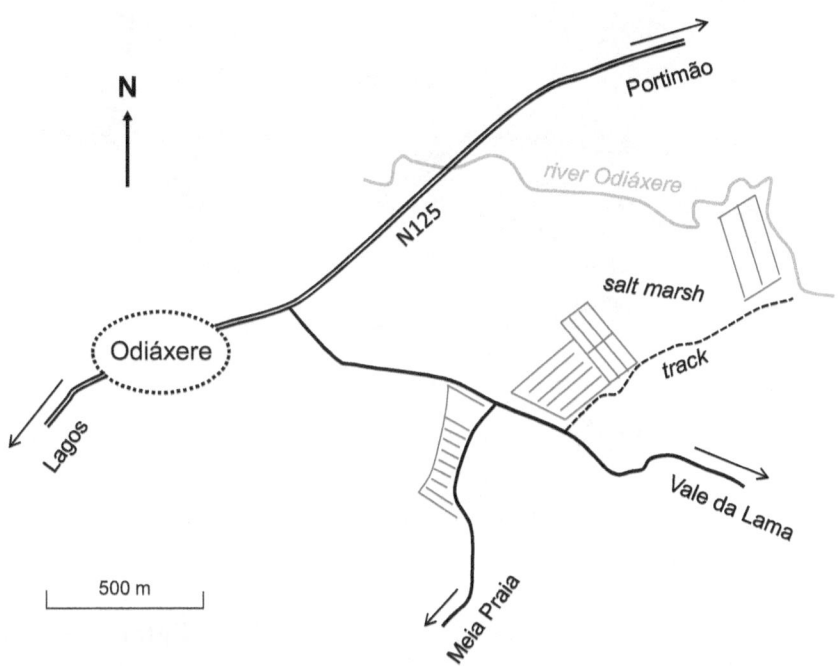

In the saltpans themselves, it is possible to see several species of waders, as well as Grey Heron, Little Egret, Spoonbill and sometimes Greater Flamingo and Glossy Ibis. This is also a good place to see Water Pipit, which in autumn and winter can be found both in the saltpans and in the saltmarsh.

Black-winged Kite is often seen hunting in the surrounding fields, while Marsh Harrier turns up occasionally. Other land birds commonly seen around here include Crested Lark, Zitting Cisticola, Iberian Magpie, Linnet and the exotic Waxbill. In spring and summer, this area attracts many swifts and hirundines, which come here to feed.

Don't miss the interesting colony of White Stork on the south side of the N125, just east of Odiáxere. Nests have been built on very low olive trees, close to the road.

17

Vale da Lama

An estuarine area with mudflats, saltmarsh and dunes.

Birds

Resident: Little Egret, Kentish Plover, Crested Lark, Zitting Cisticola, Sardinian Warbler, Iberian Magpie, Spotless Starling, Linnet

Breeding visitors: Little Tern, Bee-eater, Red-rumped Swallow

Non-breeding visitors: Gannet, Cormorant, Osprey, Oystercatcher, Ringed Plover, Common Redshank, Greenshank, Common Sandpiper, Sanderling, Dunlin, Bar-tailed Godwit, Whimbrel, Turnstone, Mediterranean Gull, Black-headed Gull, Audouin's Gull, Lesser Black-backed Gull, Sandwich Tern, Caspian Tern, Black Tern, Kingfisher

How to visit it

The best way to get there is to follow the N125 to Odiáxere and then turn right towards Vale da Lama. Pass the saltpans (described on page 16) and proceed until the railway line appears on the left side of the road. An unsurfaced and rather bumpy track crosses the railway line and will take you to the edge of the estuary (37.1336, -8.6245).

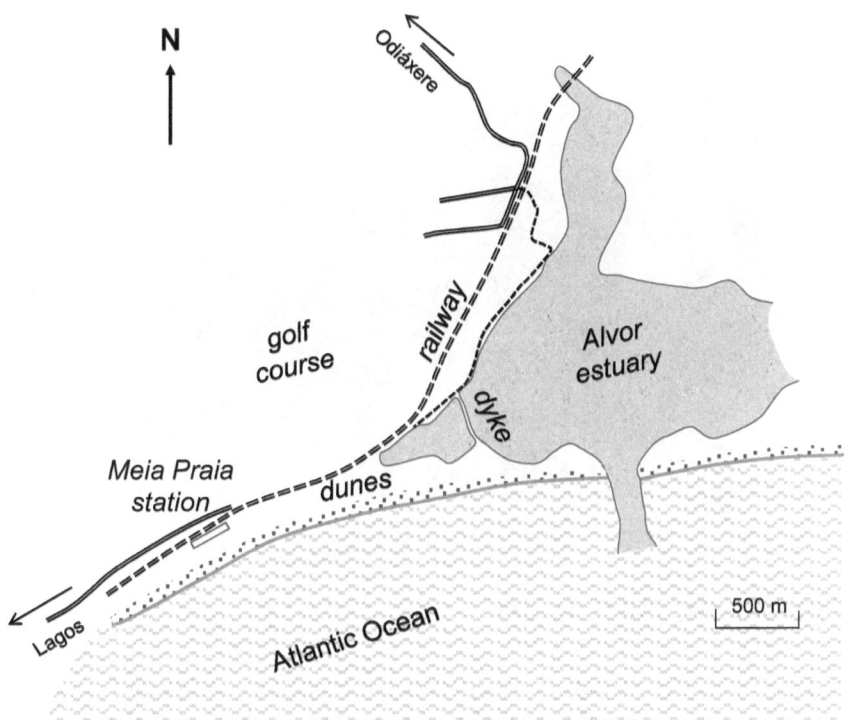

Birding in this area is better in the afternoon, when the sunlight is coming from the west. However, high tide should be avoided, as the water level may be too high and the birds may be roosting elsewhere.

When the tide is low, there are usually many birds roosting on the sandbanks or feeding on the mudflats. A scan of the estuary usually produces a good variety of waterbirds, namely waders, gulls and terns. Little Tern is frequent in summer, while Caspian Tern is regular in winter.

Carrying on for another km, the track ends near a small pond, which is separated from the estuary by a dyke. This place usually has good numbers of Mediterranean Gulls in winter, as well as a few waders and Little Egret.

A path runs along the dyke and leads to the dunes. From here it is possible to scan the sandbanks and search for waterbirds. The dunes hold Crested Lark and Zitting Cisticola, but other species put in an appearance on migration. It is also worthwhile taking a look at the sea.

Barão de São João

A large patch of woodland, consisting mainly of wattles and pines. At the top there is a wind farm, which is clearly visible in the distance.

Birds

Resident: Iberian Green Woodpecker, Great Spotted Woodpecker, Thekla's Lark, Woodlark, Mistle Thrush, Dartford Warbler, Sardinian Warbler, Crested Tit, Short-toed Treecreeper, Serin, Cirl Bunting, Rock Bunting, Corn Bunting

Breeding visitors: Short-toed Eagle, Turtle Dove, Cuckoo, Woodchat Shrike

Non-breeding visitors: soaring birds, Crag Martin, Goldcrest, Firecrest, Siskin

How to visit it

Leave Lagos northwards on the N120. When reaching Portelas, turn left towards Barão de São João and follow this road for 8 km. Upon reaching the village, look for signs reading 'Mata Nacional'. A large unpaved road will take you uphill, first through exotic wattles and then among Umbrella Pines. After about 2 km, one reaches the top (37.1481, -8.7911), which is marked by a trig point. Here it is possible to park and walk around. Several tracks run through the woods and can be used to explore the area. It is also possible to drive southwards, on a large track that runs along the wind farm.

The pinewoods hold several forest birds, including Woodlark, Firecrest, Crested Tit, Short-toed Treecreeper and Rock Bunting.

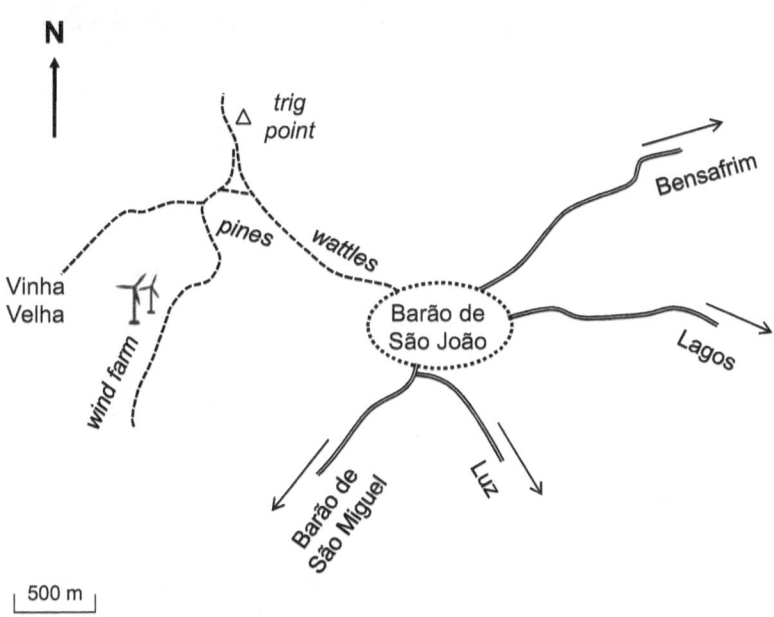

The western slope, towards Vinha Velha (signposted) leads to an open valley, where it is possible to find several open country species, including Thekla's Lark, Woodlark and Corn Bunting.

Many soaring birds have been recorded in autumn, including Black Stork, Griffon and Egyptian Vultures and Booted and Bonelli's Eagles.

Windy days should be avoided, as the noise from the wind farm can be quite annoying.

Catalão

A transition area between the hills to the north and the coastal lowlands to the south. Lightly wooded with almond, carob, fig and olive trees. There are also a few agricultural fields.

Birds

Resident: Quail, Cattle Egret, Black-winged Kite, Kestrel, Stone Curlew, Little Owl, Hoopoe, Iberian Green Woodpecker, Thekla's Lark, Woodlark, Zitting Cisticola, Sardinian Warbler, Southern Grey Shrike, Iberian Magpie, Spotless Starling, Serin, Corn Bunting

Breeding visitors: Pallid Swift, Alpine Swift, Bee-eater, Red-rumped Swallow, Woodchat Shrike

Non-breeding visitors: Skylark, Crag Martin, Meadow Pipit, Black Redstart

How to visit it

From Lagos, take the N120 northwards and turn left at Portelas, following signs to 'Barão de São João'. After about 4 km, shortly after passing Monte Judeu and the crossroads to Bensafrim, there is a narrow road to the left signposted 'Catalão'.

This road passes a small group of houses and eventually turns into a track. A trig point on a nearby hill is a great spot from where to look around (37.1268, -8.7484). In autumn this place is a good vantage point to search for raptors.

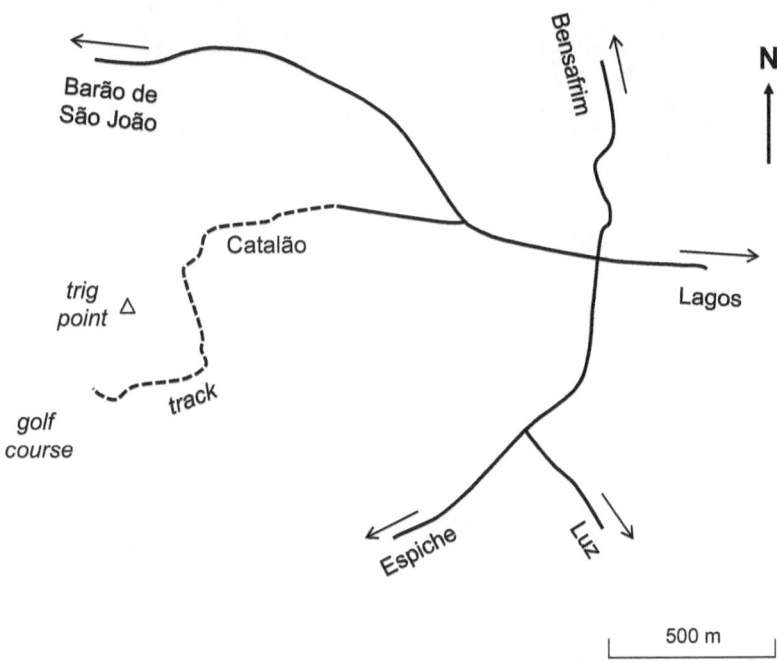

Several aerial lines run through the area and they are worth inspecting, as they are often used as a perch by Black-winged Kite, Kestrel and Southern Grey Shrike.

The more open sectors are good places to look for larks. Thekla's is regular here and can most easily be identified by its song and calls. Woodlark is usually present and small flocks can sometimes be seen, whereas Skylark occurs in winter.

Other birds that can often be seen in the fields include Stone-Curlew (a very scarce species around Lagos), Quail, Zitting Cisticola and Corn Bunting.

Pincho

A hilly area in the southern half of the Serra de Espinhaço de Cão. It consists mainly of cork oak forest, riparian woodland and scrub.

Birds

Resident: Tawny Owl, Great Spotted Woodpecker, Woodlark, Dartford Warbler, Sardinian Warbler, Firecrest, Long-tailed Tit, Nuthatch, Short-toed Treecreeper, Serin, Cirl Bunting, Rock Bunting

Breeding visitors: Short-toed Eagle, Turtle Dove, Cuckoo, Red-rumped Swallow, Nightingale, Common Redstart, Melodious Warbler, Iberian Chiffchaff

Non-breeding visitors: Crag Martin, Siskin, Bullfinch

How to visit it

To get there, leave Lagos northwards on the N120 towards Aljezur. 5 km after passing Bensafrim, next to km 160, turn right where a sign reads Pincho and park (37.1965, -8.7604). The location is best explored on foot.

Several small streams flow through this place. It is worth taking a look at the riparian woodland, which in spring has Nightingale, Melodious Warbler and Iberian Chiffchaff, whereas Bullfinch occurs in autumn and winter. This habitat is also good to look for Long-tailed Tit – birds here belong to the subspecies *irbii*, which has a grey back.

The best patches of cork oak lie to the west of the N120 and can be approached using a track that leads westwards. Here it is possible to find Woodlark, Short-toed Treecreeper, Cirl Bunting and Rock Bunting. This is one of the very few spots in the western Algarve where Common Redstart can be seen during the breeding season. Tawny Owl also occurs in the woods.

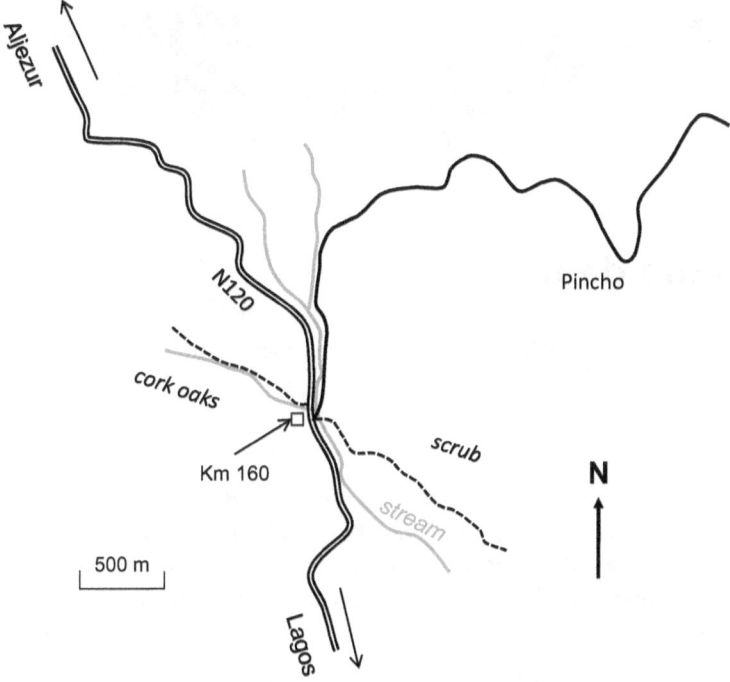

On the right side of the road, another track, signposted 'Sernada', leads to an area of extensive scrub, mainly Gum Rockrose. Dartford Warbler is quite common here.

It is also possible to explore on foot along the minor road to Pincho. This road runs along the edge of the cork oak woodland, then bends to the right and the trees give way to scrubby hillsides. Eventually one reaches Pincho, which is a small hamlet in the middle of the hills.

Bravura dam

A reservoir in the hills, surrounded by scrub and plantations of pine and eucalyptus.

Birds

Resident: Little Egret, Iberian Green Woodpecker, Great Spotted Woodpecker, Thekla's Lark, Woodlark, Crag Martin, Grey Wagtail, Black Redstart, Blue Rock Thrush, Dartford Warbler, Sardinian Warbler, Long-tailed Tit, Serin, Cirl Bunting, Rock Bunting, Corn Bunting

Breeding visitors: Short-toed Eagle, Turtle Dove, Red-rumped Swallow, Nightingale, Subalpine Warbler

Non-breeding visitors: Dunnock, Firecrest, Siskin

How to visit it

This place lies about 10 km north of Lagos. Access is via Odiáxere, following the signs to 'Barragem da Bravura'. The road passes under the motorway A22 and then through the tiny village of Cotifo. About

3 km ahead, the reservoir appears and the road ends. It is possible to park and explore on foot (37.2011, -8.6994).

The reservoir itself is not particularly interesting, as its waters are very deep and thus of little use to waterbirds. Apart from the odd Grey Heron, Little Egret or Cormorant, there are very few waterbirds here.

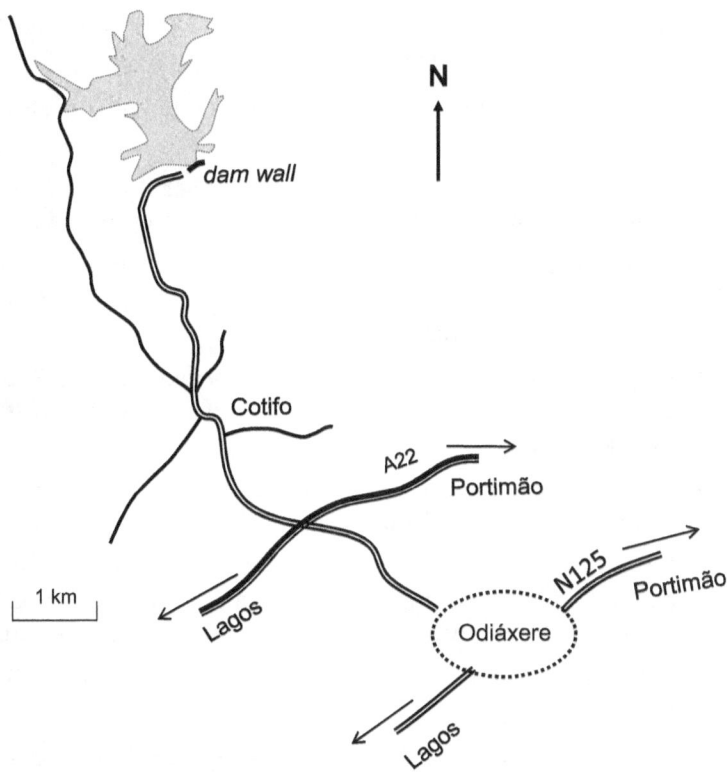

However, the surroundings are worth inspecting. From the car park, it is possible to walk down to the dam wall, where Crag Martins occur year-round. Other passerines that can often be seen there include Grey Wagtail, Blue Rock Thrush and Rock Bunting.

The slope near the dam wall is covered by bushes and a small pine plantation. Here it is possible to find Great Spotted Woodpecker, Nightingale, Serin and sometimes Long-tailed Tit.

The road between the reservoir and Cotifo passes an area of scrub with a few trees and open fields; this sector is good for Short-toed Eagle, larks and warblers, including Subalpine and Dartford.

Using public transport

For those without a car, it is still possible to get to most hotspots described here using public transport.

The Lagos bus network is called 'A ONDA'; timetables and ticket prices can be checked online at http://aonda.pt/

The following list provides some tips about how to get to each hotspot. All buses leave from the town centre.

- Ponta da Piedade – take bus line number 2 towards Porto de Mós, get out at Torraltinha and then walk southwards.

- Lagos harbour – this place lies close to the city centre and can be easily reached by crossing over the pedestrian bridge located just south of the marina.

- Lagos marsh – the southern part is served by lines 3, 5 and 8, which stop not far from the airfield; the northern part is served by line 5 only.

- Odiáxere salt pans – line number 3 to Odiáxere, then walk south-eastwards for 1 km.

- Vale da Lama – line 2 runs to Meia Praia railway station (it is also possible to get there by train from Lagos); from here, walk eastwards for 10 min until you reach the shore of the estuary.

- Barão de São João – line number 6 runs from Lagos to Barão de São João village.

- Catalão – line 7 stops at the eastern edge of this location.

- Pincho – this location is not served by the Lagos bus network; however, EVA has a bus service linking Lagos with Aljezur that runs through the area and stops near the crossroad mentioned in the text.

- Bravura dam – there are no buses to the dam wall, however line number 8 links Lagos to Cotifo; from here it is possible to walk to the dam (3 km).